DATE			

The Library of Liberal Arts

THE POEMS OF SAPPHO

THE POEMS OF SAPPHO

Translated, with an Introduction, by

SUZY Q. GRODEN

THE LIBRARY OF LIBERAL ARTS

published by

THE BOBBS-MERRILL COMPANY, INC.
INDIANAPOLIS

PA
4408
.E5
.G7

Eleven of these poems first appeared,
in slightly different form, in *Arion*,
Volume III, No. 3 © 1964 by *Arion*,
and are reprinted by permission.

The Bobbs-Merrill Company, Inc.
4300 West 62nd Street
Indianapolis, Indiana 46268

First Edition
Third Printing—1975

Library of Congress Catalog Card Number: 65–26542
ISBN 0–672–60464–7 (pbk.)

This book is dedicated to my father.

PREFACE

I wish to thank Professor G. M. Kirkwood of Cornell University for reading these translations and making invaluable suggestions for their necessary revision. It is an honor to have been guided, even briefly, by a man of such stature, and to have had the benefit of his acute sensitivity to the poetry, his attention to detail, and his profound knowledge of the text.

I also wish to thank Professor Konrad Gries of Queens College for having helped me to get started in this work. Our early studies of the fragments remained a constant aid to me in the later work.

It is almost impossible for me to express my deep gratitude to Professor Ursula Schoenheim of Queens College for her continuous support, guidance, and instruction during my work on these translations. It is safe to say that they could hardly have existed were it not for her, and there is no way to measure the patience and energy with which she read the translations and offered suggestions for their improvement.

S. Q. G.

Cambridge, Massachusetts
September 1965

CONTENTS

INTRODUCTION

To read Sappho is to invoke the majesty of time and an awareness of mortality. The fragments that have survived the centuries as lines of words torn from context have a special beauty and poignance for that very reason. Their music is inextricably interwoven with the sadness of a lost past.

Sappho lived during the late seventh and early sixth centuries B.C. She was born at Mytilene or Eresus on the island of Lesbos, and is considered to have been of good, perhaps aristocratic, family. From various sources, mostly late but including Herodotus, the following biographical information can be put together: She was said to have been the daughter of a father named Scamandronymus[1] and a mother named Cleïs; the sister of three brothers, Charaxus, Larichus, and Erigyius; the wife of a man from Andros named Cercylas; and the mother of a daughter named Cleïs.

During her lifetime Lesbos was in a state of political turmoil, and when the commoner Pittacus came to power, Sappho and others of the aristocratic party may have been forced to leave the island to live as exiles in Sicily.

Virtually nothing further is known about the details of her life. Her poetry indicates that she was surrounded by a circle of admiring young girls, most probably in the same way that Socrates was surrounded by a circle of young men. In the same spirit she was a teacher or leader of this group, and

---

[1] According to Suidas (Lexicon), Sappho's father's name is in doubt. The possibilities mentioned are Simon, Eunominus, Eurygyus, Ecrytus, Semus, Scamandronymus, Scamon, and Euarchus.

possibly she helped the girls to develop their poetic and social skills, although she must have done so in an unofficial capacity, for a member of the aristocracy could not have held any such formal position.

Despite the lack of explicit reference in the poetry, there can be little doubt that the feelings of devotion and passion that seem to have characterized Sappho's relationships with these girls had some sort of erotic expression; in fact, it seems reasonable to suppose that the very fragmentary state of the extant works is to some extent the result of the misguided zeal of scribes who deleted and altered lines that expressed something offensive to them, if they did not neglect the work altogether, as was their wont.

To most people the name Sappho is not unknown. This does not mean, however, that most people know who Sappho was. In the 2,600 years since she lived, her reputation has fluctuated wildly, although it has never totally died. The world has always thought something about Sappho, but its opinions have varied to such an extent that they could give rise to a suggestion like that of Aelian, who wrote that there were two Sapphos, one the renowned poetess, the other a notorious courtesan.

During her own lifetime Sappho's work was valued highly. There exists a tradition that Solon of Athens said he wished only to learn a certain poem of Sappho's and then die. Although the story is very unlikely, its mere existence indicates something of Sappho's importance to the ancients. The *Palatine Anthology* ascribes to Plato (among others) an elegiac couplet in which she is referred to as a tenth muse. Nevertheless, it is possible that the open-hearted passion and simplicity of her works embarrassed and alarmed the sophisticated Greeks of the fourth century B.C., so that she became a figure to be mocked and satirized in Middle Comedy, her reputation becoming one of licentiousness and immorality. However great she was thought to be by poets like Horace, the impression created by those burlesques persisted. Some scholars of the nineteenth century tried to whitewash her sullied image, arguing too far in the other direction, from evidence read into the few fragments in their possession. They set her up as a model of sober morality, as the priestess-leader of a θίασος or religious cult group.

A great many legends became attached to Sappho's name concerning various love affairs with both men and women. Her name has been linked romantically with many of the great lyric poets of Greece, including Alcaeus, the other famous poet of Lesbos, who was her contemporary; but most of the men mentioned as her lovers lived long before or after her. She was said to have died a tragic death in a "lover's leap" from the Rock of Leucas for the sake of a mysterious boatman named Phaon, who is not mentioned in any of the poems we have. To a great extent, these stories amount to just so much ornamental nonsense, invented centuries after Sappho's death because, for some reason, the poetry alone did not satisfy readers who needed an accompanying jungle of fictitious background material.

Possibly, however, modern readers will be more willing to approach the work by itself, and will prefer the heightened intensity resulting from the fact that the lines are surrounded by mysterious blanks. The isolation of the fragments sets the poetry in a kind of minor key. One seems to be hearing faint snatches of a human voice, coming up through a vast chasm of deep silence.

There is no way of knowing what the lost poems were like, or what place the single words and lines that are not lost might have occupied in a complete poem. The extant work of Sappho seems to indicate that she wrote almost entirely for herself and her immediate circle of friends. Her poems are personal to an extent that is almost unparalleled in ancient literature. It is not merely a matter of her not being a "metaphysical" or "political" poet. Although she demonstrates a great understanding of human nature, she does not seem to be concerned with extending her observations on the immediate situation to a more general level. She never says, "This is Life as I see it"; she is content to say, "This is exactly how it was then, and this is how it is now, and it looks so and I feel so and I am and you are." In these fragments Sappho appears to wish only to grasp and display the reality of her world, to focus her vision on the minute details of her life and emotions. Her purpose is to set things down as beautifully as she can, not to interpret them or to presume any understanding of them beyond the aesthetic. The only judgment she makes on all the reality with which she deals is the declaration that it is bad to make her suffer and good to give her joy. One detects here the pressure of an immense energy concentrated on the achievement of an accurate expression of the poet's self, constantly seeking a truer apprehension of the immediate and the actual.

Sappho's poetry is classed as "melic" or true lyric. Such poetry is made up of lines that vary in length but comprise uniformly patterned stanzas (the word μέλος originally meant "member"); it was composed to be sung to the accompaniment of instruments and dancing. Melic poetry can exist either as monody, that is, solo lyric, or as choral lyric, as found in some of Sappho's epithalamia, or wedding songs.

The Alexandrians, who had access to much more of Sappho's poetry than we, divided her work into nine books, according to meter, but we have so little of any of these nine that we may only speculate as to the true nature of most of the material that originally went to make them up. Apparently the first book was composed solely of poems in the so-called Sapphic meter, which is hendecasyllabic and was to be revived with great success by Horace and Catullus centuries later. Here is an example of the meter, as it is used in poem 1:

$$\_ \smile \_ \smile \ \_ \smile \smile \ \_ \ \smile \_ \_$$
ποικιλοθρον' αθανατ' Αφροδιτα,

$$\_ \ \smile\_ \ \smile \_ \ \smile \smile \ \_ \smile \_ \ \_$$
παι Διος δολοπλοκε, λισσομαι σε,

$$\_ \ \smile \_ \smile \_ \ \smile\smile\_ \smile \ \_ \ \_$$
μη μ' ασαισι μηδ' ονιαισι δαμνα,

$$\_ \ \smile\smile \ \_ \_$$
ποτνια, θυμον,

As will be observed from this scansion, only three of the four lines that make up a stanza in this meter are actually hendecasyllabic. The fourth is pentasyllabic.

There is one complete poem, number 1, and it is possible to conclude from it, and also from the fairly complete poem 8, that the other poems of the first book originally had several uniform stanzas, each four lines long, and that the last line of each stanza had the metrical pattern $\_ \smile \smile \_ \_$. The second book was devoted to poems in so-called dactylic pentameter, as, for instance, poem 25:

$$\_ \smile \ \_ \ \ \smile \smile \_ \ \_ \ \smile \ \ \smile \ \_ \ \smile \_$$
ηραμαν μεν εγω σεθεν, Ατθι, παλαι ποτα . . .

$$\_ \ \_ \ \_ \ \smile\smile \_ \ \smile \ \ \smile \_ \ \smile \_$$
σμικρα μοι παις εμμεν' εφαινεο καχαρις.

The third was made up of poems in Asclepiads or, more accurately, Greater Asclepiads (which are longer by one choriamb than Lesser Asclepiads). Here is poem 30, comprising a single line of scannable Greek:

$$\smile\smile \_\smile\smile \ \_ \ \_ \ \smile\smile \_ \ \_ \smile \ \smile\_ \ \smile \ \_$$
βροδοπαχεες αγναι Χαριτες δευτε Διος κοραι

Each of the other books seems to have included poems in a variety of meters, but their remains are too fragmentary to permit many acceptable reconstructions.

Book nine, including poems 47 through 61, is taken by most scholars to be made up of epithalamia.

The diction of the poetry is one of its most striking characteristics. It is simple, almost conversational, and repetitive.

One can go through the poems and find that certain key words recur constantly, providing both an indication of Sappho's own personality and a unifying element for the entire body of work. They are all words evoking mood, either referring to an emotion actually felt, such as desire, joy, or despair, or describing something seen in equally emotional terms, such as exquisite, delicate, lovely, desirable, sweet, rich, or tender. This repetition can be seen as deliberate and is often extremely effective in creating a rhythmical pattern of association, or in drawing an implied analogy by describing two different things in the same terms. However, it is also occasionally possible to see this repetition as an indication that Sappho wrote quickly, using words as they occurred to her and, in all probability, not going back over the lines to polish, delete, add, vary. Many commentators have noted her skilled use of meter, but this could result as much from exceptional facility as from faithful devotion to the minute details of language. The nature of the poetry itself, its subject matter, its highly emotional tone, and the simplicity and honesty of its revelations would seem to support this view, at least much of the time.

If much of this poetry was actually "dashed off," in this fact may be found its greatnesses and its faults. Perhaps the chief fault is the monotony which threatens to result from Sappho's constant attention to herself. In Greek it is possible to emphasize a word by placing it strategically in a line; the first and last words are particularly prominent. It is also possible to make a word stand out by surrounding it with others that are unrelated to it. In Sappho's poetry, the one word that appears most often in such prominence is ἐγώ, that is, "I." There is no denying that a poet commonly projects his personality and actively confronts his reader through his works, and it is not unusual for this to occur on a genuinely intimate level. But in Sappho's poetry there is almost no relief from the confrontation. The reader is forced to deal with Sappho's constant assertion of herself, which can be an exhilarating experience, but is quite often an exhausting one as well.

The poetry gains considerably more from its strengths, however, than it loses from its weaknesses. Allowing for the subject matter, which is almost exclusively that of personal emotion, it is notably subtle. Sappho often turns the entire tone of a passage from one of despair or complaint to one of rueful amusement at her own expense. In poems 51, 58, 74, and 101, she berates herself for her weaknesses, and laughs at her self-dramatization. In poem 1 she shows herself in both moods, shifting from a tone of serious request in the first half to one of self-amusement in the second. She does so by mentioning, in the midst of her fervent appeal to Aphrodite, the many other times when she has made similar requests. She suggests that she can foresee a time when her present sufferings will also be comfortably in the past, and she makes fun of herself for the frequency with which she gets into such circumstances. It is a virtue of the poetry that Sappho shows herself as she changes mood, does not hold back from mocking her own intensity of emotion, and is able to shake her head over her own foolishness. Furthermore, Sappho displays her most intimate sensations with a precision that creates a sense of reserve. By finding the perfect description for a feeling, she manages to assign it a kind of reality which is, because of its detail, more specific and more intense than that of daily life. Often a poet must be somewhat removed from his subject in order to deal with it most clearly, and the very exactness of Sappho's art serves, more effectively than vagueness could, to set apart from her the thing or feeling described.

Although Sappho uses almost no true metaphors, she chooses her similes meticulously, with the result that they have remained profoundly moving expressions, even in their fragmentary form. A typical instance of this is found in poem 48:

$$οἶον τὸ γλυκύμαλον ἐρεύθεται ἄκρῳ ἐπ' ὔσδῳ,$$
$$ἄκρον ἐπ' ἀκροτάτῳ, λελάθοντο δὲ μαλοδρόπηες,$$
$$οὐ μὰν ἐκλελάθοντ', ἀλλ' οὐκ ἐδύναντ' ἐπίκεσθαι^2$$

Sappho is perhaps comparing a bride to an apple, and in this brief simile she manages to mention all the qualities that make the girl desirable, while maintaining the subtlety that gives the fragment its charm. She implies the blushing girl by speaking of reddening fruit, and suggests at the same time the bride's fresh, youthful ripeness. Moreover, she suggests the girl's high social and moral standing by extending her simile to describe the apple's height on the tree, implying that both girl and fruit are more desirable for their elusiveness.

The power of most of the fragments lies in their ability to create a mood in a matter of one or two lines. Sappho often uses memory to this end, as a force that can bind others to her. In many of the fragments her device is to recall the past for her readers, stirring their senses with the mention of sounds, smells, feelings that she knows they have experienced.

The sense of urgency and energy that pervades much of the poetry results from its being like snatches of direct conversation, not in the way that dialogue written for the theater seems like conversation, but as if the fragments were actual messages to someone Sappho knew. This resemblance to real conversation should not lead the reader to assume a lack of skill in Sappho's use of the more conventional poetic devices

---

[2] . . . like the sweet-apple
  that has reddened
  at the top of a tree,
  at the tip of the topmost bough,
  and the apple pickers
  missed it there—no, not missed, so much
  as could not touch . . .

and techniques. Her work provides ample evidence of such skill. For example, the alliteration in the translation of poem 2 is an attempt to substitute for the internal consonance of the original, in which Sappho combines a repetition of *d* sounds—

ἐν δ' ὕδωρ ψῦχρον κελάδει δι' ὕσδων³

(en d' udōr psuchron keladei di' usdōn)

—to imitate the soft, patterned sound of the water in a brook, with that of onomatopoeic *s* sounds in the lines following—

βρόδοισι δὲ παῖς ὁ χῶρος
ἐσκίαστ', αἰθυσσομένων δὲ φύλλων⁴

(brodoisi de païs o chōros
eskiast', aithussomenōn de phullōn)

—suggesting the wind in the leaves that she is describing. The repetition of words and images, mentioned before as characteristic of Sappho's style, is often used consciously as a device. She achieves the mood she is seeking by establishing a pattern of sound through repetition that is almost a verbal gesture—that is, she imitates with words, the matter of her lines. For instance, in poem 47a she does this in a deceptively simple two-line fragment:

Ἔσπερε πάντα φέρων ὅσα φαίνολις ἐσκέδασ' Αὔως,
†φέρεις ὄιν, φέρεις αἶγα, φέρεις ἄπυ† μάτερ, παῖδα.⁵

(Espere panta pherōn osa phainolis eskedas' Auōs,
†phereis oin, phereis aiga, phereis aput materi paida.)

³ and cool water rustles through the (apple) shoots.
⁴ All the place is shadowed with roses
    and (deep sleep slips down) through the shimmering leaves.
⁵ Evening Star, you bring back
    all that was scattered
    in the shimmer of Dawn.
    You bring the sheep, you bring the goat, and
    you bring her child to the mother.

The first line describes the primary gesture, the scattering of all things into the day by the dawn; the second represents the contrapuntal, answering gesture, the gathering back of these things by the evening star. The first line is a masterpiece of effective use of word order. The two forces, Hesperus and Eos, are set against each other as the first and last words. The line breaks into halves, with one verb, "bring," and its subject, the Evening Star, in the first half, and another verb, "scatter," with Dawn, in the second. This division is saved from being overly obvious by the inclusion of the word φαίνολις ("shimmer"), a word which technically modifies Αὔως ("Dawn"), yet can suggest at the same time the light of the star. In the second line, which describes and almost acts out the gathering back, although Sappho does not specifically mention a shepherd, she creates an image of the Evening Star as one by naming the creatures he gathers, a sheep and a goat; and here the repetition of the word φέρεις suggests the physical action of gathering things up, which is usually performed rhythmically, like the repeated gesture of pulling in a length of rope, or stooping and reaching to pick up scattered objects. Although this obviously was not the end of the original poem, the climactic word order of this second line makes the fragment seem somehow complete. After the image of the Evening Star as a shepherd has been established, Sappho again repeats that "gesture-word," φέρεις, and at the end of the line sets the word that is the essential subject of the poem: the child, who must be shepherded home to her mother. Unfortunately, as the daggers in the text indicate, the correctness of most of this line is in serious doubt, so that its skill cannot confidently be attributed to Sappho's talent.

Lobel and Page include nearly two hundred fragments in their text of the works of Sappho. For several reasons a number of them have been omitted from this translation. The most important and most frequently applicable is that the text is simply too fragmentary to permit accurate understanding and translation. Since Greek word order is largely arbitrary, and any word may conceivably occur any place, the absence of a word from a line could rob that line of its meaning or distort it considerably. For this reason those fragments which consist of partial lines, lacking beginnings, ends, or middles, have been omitted. This is not to say that the sense of a fragment cannot seem to be quite clear despite its tattered condition, and many translations contain versions of a poem that would seem to assume that what is there is all that needs to be. Some editors have even felt that it was possible to complete poems, and often a familiar "Sapphic" poem turns out to be the work of a modern editor; by adding his own beginnings, ends, and middles to the partial lines that are actually Sappho's, he created a new poem. In dealing with expository prose works this sort of editorial activity may sometimes be worth while, for the sense of such writings is of primary value to modern readers. The value of poetry, however, lies in the poet's manipulation of minute and subtle details of language, and it is historically meaningless to reconstruct what has been lost. In matters of such delicacy, to miss the original by a single nuance is usually to miss the major value of the entire poem. In finishing some broken lines or stanzas, a sensitive and imaginative editor may produce good poetry, but it is nevertheless not the original, and therefore no such reconstructions are included here.

Many of the fragments considered to have been written by Sappho have come down to us because they occur as quotations in the letters, journals, and treatises of later authors. In some cases the nature of these passages suggests that they may actually be paraphrases rather than exact quotations, and there is no way of knowing whether they are Sappho's words or someone else's version of them. Some editors have taken phrases of this sort and set them in direct speech, ignoring the "Sappho says that . . ." which precedes them, and arranging them in metrically probable lines. This, again, is dangerous, for there are many ways in which such lines may be corrupt; for this reason most such phrases have been omitted from the present translation.

On the other hand, the reader will find in this translation some fragments that might justly have been left out, according to the principles stated above. However, at the risk of appearing inconsistent, I have included them either because they were so well known that they seemed to demand consideration, or because the guesses of various editors seemed so similar and feasible that the fragments could be taken as they appeared in the text. There is no denying that where such fragments are included the possibility of error must be recognized. However, only a few such fragments have been translated here; it is hoped that they will not cause confusion for the reader.

The poems of this translation will be found to lack formal meter. Greek meter is based primarily on quantity, on the length of time it takes to say a syllable. English meter, however, is based on stress, on the relative strength with which a syllable is said. English poetry has no exact equivalent of the Greek concept, and no attempt has been made to make do with an inexact one. It seemed preferable to set out the words, ideas, and images of the original as clearly as possible in their translated form, arranging them in such a way that they might create visually some of the effects of stress and relationship that were achieved by sound and word order in the Greek. It is hoped, however, that the language of the English translation is not totally lacking in rhythm and balance.

SUZY Q. GRODEN

CONCORDANCE

L P = Edgar Lobel and Denys Page (eds.). *Poetarum Lesbiorum Fragmenta*. Oxford: Clarendon Press, 1963.

E = J. M. Edmonds (ed., trans.). *Lyra Graeca*, Volume I. Cambridge: Harvard University Press; London: William Heinemann Ltd., 1958.

SQG	LP	E	SQG	LP	E
1	1	1	22	46	56
2	2	4, 6	23	47	54
3	5	36	24	48	89
4	15	37	25	49	48
5	16	38	26	50	58
6	26	13	27	51	52
7	30	47	28	25 (Incertum)	142
8	31	2	29	52	53
9	32	10	30	53	68
10	33	9	31	54	69
11	34	3	32	55	71
12	35	5	33	56	72
13	36	23	34	57	98
14	37	17, 18	35	58	118
15	38	27	36	63	Appendix 118B
16	39	20	37	81b	117
17	40	7	38	82a	115
18	41	14	39	91	116
19	42	16	40	94	83
20	44	66	41	16 (Incertum)	114
21	45	50	42	Omitted	111

SQG	LP	E	SQG	LP	E
43	95	85	77	133	125, 126
44	96	86,	78	134	123
		Appendix 86A	79	135	122
45	98	Omitted	80	136	138
46	102	135	81	137	Alcaeus 124,
47	104	149, 32			Sappho 119
48	105a	150	82	138	120
49	105c	151	83	140a	103
50	106	148	84	141	146
51	107	159	85	142	140
52	108	157	86	143	139
53	109	153	87	144	55
54	110a	154	88	145	78
55	111	148	89	146	106
56	112	155, 156, 158	90	147	76, 77
57	113	163	91	148	100
58	114	164	92	149	141
59	115	161	93	150	108
60	116	162	94	151	141A
61	117	160	95	152	21
62	118	80	96	153	102
63	119	131	97	154	112
64	Omitted	144	98	155	121
65	120	74	99	156	59, 60
66	121	99	100	157	177
67	122	107	101	158	137
68	123	19	102	159	75
69	124	127	103	160	12
70	126	128	104	161	Omitted
71	127	129	105	162	132
72	128	101	106	163	29
73	129	124, 22	107	164	79
74	130	81	108	165	26
75	131	81	109	166	97
76	132	130	110	167	62

SQG	LP	E	SQG	LP	E
111	168	25	123	181	182
112	169	183	124	182	183
113	171	173	125	184	184
114	172	28	126	185	30
115	173	174	127	186	185
116	174	175	128	187	186
117	175	176	129	188	28
118	176	178	130	189	187
119	177	179	131	190	188
120	178	95	132	191	64
121	179	180	133	192	191
122	180	181			

SELECTED BIBLIOGRAPHY

Bowra, Sir Cecil M. *Greek Lyric Poetry*. Oxford: Clarendon Press, 1961.

Edmonds, J. M. (ed., trans.). *Lyra Graeca*. Vol. I. "Loeb Classical Library." Cambridge: Harvard University Press, 1958.

Halporn, James W., Martin Ostwald, and Thomas G. Rosenmeyer. *The Meters of Greek and Latin Poetry*. Indianapolis and New York: The Bobbs-Merrill Company, Inc., 1963.

Lobel, Edgar, and Denys Page (eds.). *Poetarum Lesbiorum Fragmenta*. Oxford: Clarendon Press, 1963.

Moore, J. A. (ed.). *Selections from the Greek Elegiac, Iambic and Lyric Poets*. Cambridge: Harvard University Press, 1947.

Page, Denys. *Sappho and Alcaeus: An Introduction to the Study of Ancient Lesbian Poetry*. Oxford: Clarendon Press, 1959.

Robinson, David M. *Sappho and Her Influence*. Boston: Marshall Jones & Co., 1924.

Smyth, Herbert Weir (ed.). *Greek Melic Poets*. New York: Biblo and Tannen, 1963.

*Treu, Max (ed., trans.). *Sappho*. Munich: Ernst Heimeran, 1958.

Weigall, Arthur. *Sappho of Lesbos: Her Life and Times*. New York: Stokes, 1932.

---

* The translator is not personally familiar with this book but has included it in the Bibliography because it is considered the most reliable German translation and because it includes a very full bibliography of publications on Sappho in a wide variety of languages.

TRANSLATOR'S NOTE

In a few cases fragments that Lobel and Page have omitted, or relegated to a special section for fragments of uncertain authorship, have been translated here. They have been included because they were too well known to be ignored.

A section of notes begins on page 141. Any fragment for which a note is included is marked (*).

The mark (§) indicates that a fragment has been transmitted without Sappho's name.

SAPPHO

When she sat among the scattered writings
and diverse thoughts
she felt them
and was alone among a like throng.

They had been lovers in the past
and were as birds in April flight,
carried on sister wings
toward silent moons
to some still undiscovered place
where they would meet.

And there were feathers in her hair.
She watched those birds that flew so close
with eyes that haunt us still;
they are the eyes of one who wakes at dawn
to weep,
and wash away the kinder touch of dreams.

She sought the lily moon
among the branches of a willow tree
but it was gone again—
passed swiftly through the hair
of bending fibrile boughs.

She played them on their way
with whispered songs,
as still as secrets told by twigs
that shift and touch—
            (discreet and tender whips)
the branches lisping as they rub,
like slender, girlish arms.

THE POEMS OF SAPPHO

Eternal Aphrodite, rainbow-throned,
you cunning, wily child of Zeus, I beg you,
do not break me, Lady,
with the pains and raging ills of love.
But come to me, if ever in the past
you heard my far-off cries
and heeding, came,
leaving the golden home of Zeus
in your bridled chariot.
Beautiful swift sparrows bore you,
eddying through the mid-air, their wings a-whirr,
from heaven to the dark earth,
and there they were. And you, blessed Lady,
smiling your immortal smile,
asked me what ailed me now,
and why I called again,
and what my mad heart most craved:

"Whom, Sappho,
shall I lead to be your love
this time?
Who wrongs you now?
Even if she flees you, soon she'll chase,
and if she scorns your gifts, why, she will offer hers.
And if she does not love you,
soon she'll love, although she does not want to."

Now come to me once again, and free me
from these aching sorrows. Do for my heart
what it desires, and be yourself my help and ally

(1—LP 1, E 1)

Come to me here, from Crete,
to this sacred temple of the lovely apple grove.
Your altars are fragrant here with offerings of frankincense,
and cool water rustles through the apple shoots.

All the place is shadowed with roses
and deep sleep slips down through the shimmering leaves.
In here is a meadow, with horses grazing, alive
with spring blossoms and breezes
that blow redolent.

And here may you, Cypris, pour,
with graceful charm,
your nectar, mixed with our own festive rites,
into these golden cups.

(2—LP 2, E 4,6)*

Cypris and Nereids, let my brother
come back to me unscathed.
Provide all his heart's desires.

Let him repent all the errors of his past.

Let him become a joy to his friends . . .
for . . . his enemies . . .
. . . . Let us have . . .
. . . nor one . . .

Make him desire to
do honor to his sister,
. . . . . formerly . . . and he,
suffering the . . . of wretched . . .
. . . despairs . . . .

(3—LP 5, E 36)*

Cypris, let Doricha discover
how bitter
you too can be,
and stop her
from boasting loud-mouthed
how he came a second time
to a longed-for love.

(4—LP 15, E 37)

There are those who say
an array of horsemen,
and others of marching men,
and others of ships, is
the most beautiful thing on the dark earth.

But I say it is whatever one loves.

It is very easy
to show this to all:
for Helen,
by far the most beautiful of mortals,
left her husband
and sailed to Troy
giving no thought at all
to her child nor dear parents,
but was led . . .
[by her love alone.]

Now, far away, Anactoria
comes to my mind.
For I would rather watch her
moving in her lovely way,
and see her face, flashing radiant,
than all the force of Lydian chariots,
and their infantry in full display of arms.

(5—LP 16, E 38)

... and whenever
I am good
to people,
they're the ones
who hurt me
most of all

(6—LP 26, E 13)*

. . . .
night . . .
[and] young girls . . .
the long night's watch . . .
and serenade your very-dear-and-
decked-in-periwinkle bride.

But wake up, young bachelor-boy,
go out . . . your friends . . .
. . . we shall see
just as much sleep
as [will]
the clear-voiced . . .

(7—LP 30, E 47)

An equal to the gods, he seems to me,
the man who, with his face toward yours,
sits close and listens to the whispers of
your sweet voice and enticing laugh.
To watch has made my heart a pounding hammer in my
            breast.
For as I look at you, if only for an instant,
my voice no longer comes to me.
My silent tongue is broken,
and a quick and subtle flame
runs up beneath my skin.
I lose my sense of sight, hear only drumming in my ears.
I drip cold sweat,
and a trembling chases all through me.
I am greener than the pale grass
and it seems to me that I am close to death.

Still, I must endure all this

(8—LP 31, E 2)

By teaching me their art
they honored me

(9—LP 32, E 10)*

if only,
golden-crowned Aphrodite,
such a lot would fall to
me

stars around the beautiful moon
obscure their radiance again
when, with her fullest light,
she floods all the earth

(11—LP 34, E 3)

. . . you . . . [in] either
Cyprus or Paphos or Panormus

(12—LP 35, E 5)*

I want and yearn

(13—LP 36, E 23)§

. . . about my grief . . .

and may winds blast him
who attacks [me],
and [devouring] cares

. . . you roast me . . . .

(15—LP 38, E 27)

and her feet she hid
with the many-colored thongs
they work so beautifully in Lydia

(16—LP 39, E 20)

. . . and I [made] to you
[the offering] of a white goat . . .

(17—LP 40, E 7)

my feelings for you, my beautiful ones,
will not change

(18—LP 41, E 14)§

their hearts grew chill
and they dropped their wings at their sides

(19—LP 42, E 16)*

Cyprus . . .
a herald arrived . . .
. . . a swift messenger of Ida . . .
. . . .
and the rest of Asia . . . immortal fame . . .
Hector and his fellows
are bringing home a girl with darting eyes
from holy Thebe and Placia . . .
—graceful Andromache—
with a fleet of ships, on a salt sea.
They're bringing, too, a mass of golden bracelets, and
of purple robes,
a rainbow of trinkets,
and unnumbered silver cups with ivory work.

The messenger told his tale, and Hector's
dear father jumped right up
and word spread to friends
through the wide city

At once
the sons of Ilus
fitted mules to swift-wheeled chariots,
and a whole throng of women
climbed aboard,
among them young and dainty-ankled girls,
while the daughters of Priam rode separate.
And the men harnessed their horses
to chariots,
. . . the young men . . . greatly
. . . and drivers . . .

and the sweet-strained flute was
mingled with the clattering of castanets.
The young girls sang a sacred song, and
their mighty clamor rose to the skies with sounds
of laughter.

All the road long
they carried bowls and vessels filled
with myrrh, with cinnamon and frankincense.
The older women chorused shouts,
and all the men, as one, gave out
a lovely, high-pitched chant
as they called on far-shooting Paean of the beautiful lyre

and as if to gods they sang a hymn
to Hector and Andromache.

(20—LP 44, E 66)

. . . so long as you desire . . .

(21—LP 45, E 50)

. . . and I shall lay my body
down upon a tender pillow

(22—LP 46, E 56)

Love shakes my heart
like a wind
sweeping down a mountain
onto oaks

you came
and did well in that;
I sought you.
You melted my heart,
burning with love

(24—LP 48, E 89)§*

I loved you, Atthis, long ago.
You seemed a little girl
to me,
an awkward child.

(25—LP 49, E 48)

To have beauty is to have only that,
but to have goodness
is to be beautiful
too.

(26—LP 50, E 58)

I don't know
what
to do: I am
of two minds.

(27—LP 51, E 52)

. . . and I have flown,
like a little girl
in search of her mother.

(28—LP Incertum 25, E 142)*

it is not for me, it seems,
to touch the sky
with my two arms

(29—LP 52, E 53)

Rosy-armed
Graces, come,
sacred daughters of Zeus

(30—LP 53, E 68)

. . . having come from heaven, purple-
mantled in a soldier's cape . . .

(31—LP 54, E 69)*

When you have died, there will be nothing.
No memory of you will remain,
not a trace
to linger after:
you do not share
the rose of the Muses with us,
and will wander unseen
in the hall of the dead,
a fitful shade among the blinded ghosts.

(32—LP 55, E 71)*

I do not think that any girl
who'll ever see the light of day
will have
a mind like yours

What country girl has got your mind
with trickery . . .
in her country smock,
. . . and doesn't even know
the art of drawing up her dress
about her ankles?

(34—LP 57, E 98)

But, I adore the exquisite,
and in my eyes
the love of sunlight
is both lustrous and beautiful
at once.

(35—LP 58, E 118)*

Dream . . . black . . .
you wander in and out when sleep . . .
sweet god, . . .

(36—LP 63, E Appendix 118B)*

Twine lovely garlands in your hair, my Dika,
sprigs of anise,
gathered by your soft hands.
For a plenty of flowers is by far
more dear
to the blessed Graces
who turn from those who go uncrowned

(37—LP 81b, E 117)

Mnasidika has a better figure than soft Gyrinno

No, Irana, [I] have never found you
more revolting . . .

(39—LP 91, E 116)*

. . . .
. . . and I honestly wish I were dead.
Weeping heavily, she left me,
and said, "Our anguish, Sappho,
is terribly deep—
I am really leaving you against my will."
And I answered her with this:
"Go, be happy—and
remember me—for you know
how I have cherished you,
and if you doubt it, let me call to mind for you
. . . . the beauty we shared,
the times when you would wrap around yourself,
beside me, [a profusion of garlands,]
of violets and roses, woven together . . .
and thick-plaited, sweet-smelling wreaths,
fashioned of blossoms,
you hung at your soft throat.
. . . and when you had anointed . . .
with rich and regal scents,
upon the soft bed you would fulfill your desire
for the lovely . . .
and no one . . . nor a holy . . .
. . . . that we were absent from . . .
nor a grove . . .
. . . . sound . . . .

(40—LP 94, E 83)

the Cretan women once danced thus,
elegantly,
about the lovely altar.
[And] stepping on the soft flower
of the tender grass
[they crushed the lovely things] beneath their feet

(41—LP Incertum 16, E 114)§

The moon has set,
and the Pleiades as well;
in the deep middle of the night
the time is passing,
and I lie alone.

(42—E 111)*

a desire to die
has hold of me,
and to see the shores of Acheron,
bedewed with lotus and . . .

(43—LP 95, E 85)*

. . . Sardis . . .
thinking often of us here,
of how we . . .

She saw you as a goddess
and loved your dancing so.

Now she shines among the women of Lydia
as does the rose-fingered moon when,
outshining every star,
she usurps the grandeur of the sun,
and pours her light
on saltish sea
and thickly flowered fields;

a lovely dew has filtered down,
and roses burgeon,
and the tender anthriscus
and flowering clover.

Often when she wanders,
she remembers gentle Atthis,
and, I think, her want
weighs sadness on her fine-strung heart.

. . . .
. . . for us to come there . . . .
. . . .

48

It's no easy thing for us
to match the figured beauty
of a goddess, [but] . . .
. . . you have . . .
. . . .

. . . and Aphrodite
poured her nectar from a golden . . .
. . . .
[and] . . . . Peitho
. . . in her hands

(44—LP 96, E 86, Appendix 86A)

(a)   . . . my mother [has told me]
how they used to wrap their hair
in purple ribbons in her day—
how that was quite the thing . . .

but your hair grows yellower than flame,
and you must braid it up with garlands
thick with blooms . . .

The perfect thing would be
a Sardian headband
all woven with their rainbow colors . . .

(b)   . . . but I don't know where I can get
a rainbow-colored headband
for you, Cleïs.

But . . . the Mytilenean . . .

(45—LP 98)*

Sweet mother,
I cannot, I swear, do my weaving!
I am broken in my desire for the boy,
by the tender, supple Aphrodite

(46—LP 102, E 135)

(a)   Evening Star, you bring back
all that was scattered
in the shimmer of Dawn.
You bring the sheep, you bring the goat, and
you bring her child to the mother.

(b)   . . . the most beautiful of all stars

(47—LP 104, E 149, 32)

. . . like the sweet-apple
that has reddened
at the top of a tree,
at the tip of the topmost bough,
and the apple pickers
missed it there—no, not missed, so much
as could not touch . . .

(48—LP 105a, E 150)

. . . like the hyacinth
which shepherds in the mountains
trample underfoot,
and the purple flower [lies scattered]
on the ground . . .

(49—LP 105c, E 151)§

as far superior to others
as the poet of Lesbos is
to those of other peoples

(50—LP 106, E 148)

am I still carrying a torch
for my virginity?

(51—LP 107, E 159)

oh, [my] beautiful, oh, [so very] lovely

(52—LP 108, E 157)§

"we shall give," the father said

(53—LP 109, E 153)

7 fathoms long
   (the feet of
    the doorkeeper);

5 bulls' hides
   (it took
    to make his sandals);

10 cobblers
   (to do the job).

(54—LP 110a, E 154)*

Up with the roof—
(hymenaios)

Carpenters—raise it up high—
(hymenaios)

The groom who'll enter
is as big as Ares—
Far greater
than a great big man

(55—LP 111, E 148)*

Happy bridegroom!
Now your wedding has come true,
as you have prayed, and you have
the girl for whom you prayed.
You are a joy to look at,
with your gentle eyes,

and love showers down about
your handsome face . . .
Aphrodite has honored you
above all others . . .

(56—LP 112, E 155, 156, 158)

groom, [you'll never find]
another girl like this

a bride: Childhood, my childhood, where
            are you going when you leave me?

childhood: I'll never come to you again,
            never, never.

(58—LP 114, E 164)*

What shall I make you, darling groom,
[if I'm to do you justice in my song?]

A lithe and supple bough
I'd best to
make you [in my song]

(59—LP 115, E 161)§

Be happy, bride, be very happy,
[and,] honored bridegroom . . .

Be happy, bride,
and may the groom be happy too.

(61—LP 117, E 160)§

speak, heavenly tortoise-shell,
you have the gift

.

(62—LP 118, E 80)*

· · · a dripping towel · · ·

(63—LP 119, E 131)

These are the ashes of Timas
who died before she could wed,
whom the blue-dark room of Persephone
took in instead.
And when she was dead
every girl her own age
cut, with a fresh-sharpened blade,
a beautiful lock from her head
[to lay on the grave]

(64—E 144)*

But
I'm not the spiteful sort
whose rancor festers: no,
I have a gentle, childlike heart

(65—LP 120, E 74)

Though I love you
you must find
a younger bed of love;
I cannot bear to live with you,
for I am older

a dear and delicate child,
gathering flowers

(67—LP 122, E 107)

. . . golden-slippered Dawn just now . . .

(68—LP 123, E 19)

... and you yourself, Calliope ...

(69—LP 124, E 127)

sleep in the arms of a tender friend

(70—LP 126, E 128)

come here, again, Muses,
leaving the golden . . .

(71—LP 127, E 129)

Come here,
lilting Graces, and Muses
with your lovely hair

(72—LP 128, E 101)

you have forgotten me . . .
or do you love some other man [more]
[than] you [care for] me . . . ?

(73—LP 129, E 124, 22)§

Desire shakes me once again;
here is that melting of my limbs.
It is a creeping thing, and bittersweet.
I can do nothing to resist

(74—LP 130, E 81)

you despise the thought of me,
Atthis, and fly to Andromeda

(75—LP 131, E 81)

I have a beautiful child
whose body is like golden petals.
She is my darling Cleïs
and I would not have for her
all Lydia,
nor even lovely . . .

(76—LP 132, E 130)§

now, Andromeda has got herself
a beautiful exchange . . .

Sappho, why . . .
. . . Aphrodite, who is so generous
with her blessings . . . ?

(77—LP 133, E 125, 126)

in my dream we spoke, Cyprus-born, . . .

(78—LP 134, E 123)

oh, Irana,
why . . . me,
daughter of Pandion
swallow?

(79—LP 135, E 122)*

Envoy of spring,
whose very voice
is yearning,
nightingale

(80—LP 136, E 138)

I want to say something, but
embarrassment
holds me back . . .

But if you had a desire
for what is noble and beautiful,
and your tongue weren't
stirring up evil,
embarrassment wouldn't
fill your eyes—
you'd speak out about the affair

(81—LP 137, E Alcaeus 124, Sappho 119)*

. . . stand face to face, my love,
unveil your grace before my eyes

(82—LP 138, E 120)

"Graceful Adonis is dying,
Cytherea,
what should we do?"

"Beat at your breasts, maidens,
and tear your robes."

(83—LP 140a, E 103)*

. . . there the ambrosia
had been mixed in the bowl,
and Hermes, taking up the leather flask,
poured out the drinks for the gods.
And they all
held up their drinking cups and,
pouring a libation,
prayed for every good fortune
for the bridegroom

(84—LP 141, E 146)

Leto and Niobe were deeply loving friends

(85—LP 142, E 140)

and golden pulses grew on the beach

(86—LP 143, E 139)

... completely fed up with Gorgo

(87—LP 144, E 55)

don't disturb the rubble

(88—LP 145, E 78)

no honey for me
nor honey bee

(89—LP 146, E 106)*

They will remember us
later on
I say

(90—LP 147, E 76, 77)

wealth without honor makes no harmless neighbor,
but a mixing of the two
can be the very height of joy

(91—LP 148, E 100)

(92—LP 149, E 141)

. . . when the night-long . . .
overtakes their . . .

It is not right for there to be
the sound of weeping
in a poet's home.
Such things do not become us

(93—LP 150, E 108)*

... and over their eyes
[dropped] the dark sleep of night ...

(94—LP 151, E 141A)

· · · · mingled
· · · in a profusion of colors · · ·

(95—LP 152, E 21)

sweet-voiced girl

(96—LP 153, E 102)

the moon shone full
and when the girls stood
around an altar . . .

(97—LP 154, E 112)

I bid you,
Madam Kingsblood royal,
a fond farewell . . .

(98—LP 155, E 121)*

. . . far sweeter singing
than the lyre, [and] of a
richer golden hue
than gold . . .

(99—LP 156, E 59, 60)

. . . queenly Dawn . . .

(100—LP 157, E 177)

When wrath runs rampage
in your heart,
you must hold still
that rambunctious tongue!

(101—LP 158, E 137)*

. . . you and
Love, my servant . . .

(102—LP 159, E 75)*

now I shall sing these delightful songs,
beautifully,
to my girls

(103—LP 160, E 12)

bridegrooms, you guarded
her . . . nine . . .
kings of many . . . . .

. . . with what eyes . . . ?

(105—LP 162, E 132)

... my darling ...

(106—LP 163, E 29)

she calls her child

(107—LP 164, E 79)

that fellow sees himself as . . .

(108—LP 165, E 26)

They tell of Leda's finding, once,
nestling under the thick-grown
hyacinths, an egg . . .

(109—LP 166, E 97)

so very much whiter than an egg

(110—LP 167, E 62)

oh, . . .
Adonis . . .

(111—LP 168, E 25)*

that I might lead . . .

(112—LP 169, E 183)

guileless

(113—LP 171, E 173)

bringing pain

(114—LP 172, E 28)*

of a vine
that climbs along a
pair of poles

(115—LP 173, E 174)

120

a trench

(116—LP 174, E 175)

dawn

(117—LP 175, E 176)

a lyre, a guitar,
a mandolin

(118—LP 176, E 178)*

a dress

(119—LP 177, E 179)

[like] Gello, the vampire . . .
with her overexaggerated
love for the child

(120—LP 178, E 95)

(121—LP 179, E 180)

a chest for holding ladies' things

Hector

(122—LP 180, E 181)

easily crossed

(123—LP 181, E 182)

that I might go . . .

(124—LP 182, E 183)

danger

. . . with a voice like honey

(126—LP 185, E 30)

Medea

(127—LP 186, E 185)

132

of the Muses

(128—LP 187, E 186)

weaving tales

(129—LP 188, E 28)

soap

(130—LP 189, E 187)

with vast cleverness

shoots of parsley

(132—LP 191, E 64)

golden-ankled cups

(133—LP 192, E 191)

NOTES

GLOSSARY

NOTES

2. For a long time parts of this poem were included in texts of Sappho as two unrelated fragments. Lines 3–6 of this translation were quoted by Hermogenes, in a work entitled *Kinds of Style,* to illustrate Sappho's manner of describing the sweetness and charm of a place. Lines 10–13 were known from a passage in Athenaeus' *Doctors at Dinner,* a collection of learned conversations and quotations compiled in the 3rd century A.D. However, in the 1930's a potsherd dating from the 3rd century B.C. was discovered and analyzed, and on it were engraved the 16 lines which join the two fragments as parts of an almost complete poem.

3. Herodotus, in his *Histories* II. 135, tells how a Mytilenean named Charaxus, the brother of Sappho, bought and freed the notorious courtesan Rhodopis while on a trip to Egypt. The historian goes on to say that Charaxus' sister took the occasion of his return to Mytilene to chide him in a poem, which, although written later than this, may well have had a similar tone.

6. This is a translation of lines 2–4 from a fifteen-line fragment. Since almost every other line is made up of one word, or simply parts of words, they were not included.

9. This fragment is usually taken as a reference to the Muses.

12. The poem seems to be to Aphrodite; all that is left of it are the names of three places with which she was connected.

19. In transmitting this fragment the scholiast on Pindar's *Odes* I. 10 compares Pindar's description of Zeus's eagle with Sappho's of doves.

24. The second line of the translation depends on a reading of the text that does not appear in Lobel and Page, but does in Edmonds.

28. Lobel and Page include this fragment among those of uncertain authorship because none of the sources attaches Sappho's name to it.

31. Pollux says in his *Vocabulary* X. 124 that the line refers to the god Eros.

32. Plutarch mentions this poem twice. In his *Praecepta Coniugalia* XLVIII, he says that Sappho wrote it to a wealthy woman, and in *Quaestiones Conviviales,* 3a2, he says it is to a woman of no refinement or learning. In either case the fragment shows clearly Sappho's belief in the lasting value of art and the folly of a life that lacks it.

    The text actually reads "of Pieria," rather than "of the Muses." Pieria is a district in Thessaly, with a mountain that was sacred to the Muses.

35. This is the end of a poem of at least twenty-six lines in which the myth of Eos, the dawn goddess, and Tithonus, one of her mortal lovers, occurs.

36. These are the first two and one-half of ten lines that are too fragmentary to make a coherent poem.

39. Possibly the name "Irana" was here intended to mean "Peace," which is the literal meaning of the word. If so, Sappho's statement can be interpreted quite differently, for it would then be Peace itself that she finds so revolting.

42. Lobel and Page omit this poem from their text, and Hephaestion, who quotes the passage in his *Handbook of Meter* LXX, does not attribute it directly to Sappho. Therefore, although the editors of the *Paroemiographi Graeci* (a collection of proverbs of various authors published in 1839) consider it to be by Sappho, the reader should keep in mind the strong possibility that it is not, no matter how well known it is, or how often attributed to her.

43. This is a three-line passage from a sixteen-line fragment that lacks the right-hand portion of every line. Although no real sense can be made of the text, certain words do stand out and are helpful in suggesting the poem's content. The name "Gongyla" appears as the one word of line 4, and the person whose name this is may be taken as the subject of the poem. Two lines later are the words "most of all"; and in lines 8 and 9, "oh, master" and "for . . . not . . . happy" appear, followed by "not at all . . . rejoice." Then come the three lines translated here. The poem may possibly be seen as a prayer to Eros begging him to relieve Sappho's misery over someone named Gongyla.

45. This poem is sometimes thought to have been written during Sappho's exile, to her daughter. It may refer to her inability to provide luxuries for her daughter because of the troubled times and the inconveniences of living as outcasts from Lesbos.

54. As a part of wedding celebrations it was customary to mock the bridegroom and the doorkeeper who guarded the newly-weds.

55. This fragment appears to come from a choral song probably written to be performed by attendants of the bride or bride-groom. The refrain "hymenaios" means "a wedding song" or "a wedding" and is a form of the name Hymen, the god of marriage.

58. Although there is no way to be certain, the two parts of this choral song seem to suggest a responsive recitation in which a singer would ask the first question and another, or a chorus, would answer. The fragment appears among the epithalamia, and it is reasonable to guess that at the wedding celebration for which it was written such an arrangement would have been feasible.

62. Sappho is addressing her lyre. The instrument was said to have been invented by Hermes, who stretched strings over the shell of a tortoise. The lyre did actually consist of a tortoise-

shell sounding-board with seven strings stretched across it and fastened to a bar that joined a pair of curved horns at the top.

64. This poem, which is omitted by Lobel and Page, is ascribed to Sappho in the *Palatine Anthology* VII. 489, but may well have been written by someone else. It is included here more for the sake of its fame and beauty than to assert its authenticity.

79. Sappho is probably referring to the myth of Procne, the daughter of King Pandion. The story tells how her husband, Tereus, raped her sister, Philomela, and then cut out Philomela's tongue to keep her from informing on him. Philomela, however, wove her tale of misfortune into a cloak, which she sent to Procne, whereupon Procne took revenge by killing her own son, Itys, and serving him up to his father to eat. Before Tereus could kill the sisters for their outrageous acts, the gods changed all three of them into birds.

81. Aristotle, in *Rhetoric*, 1367a, quotes lines 1–3 of the translation as the work of Alcaeus, and lines 4–10 as Sappho's answer to him. The context in which the two poems were written (if they were, in fact, two separate poems) is not known, despite the efforts of commentators to guess whether the first part was intended by Alcaeus for Sappho, whether there was some proposal involved, or whether Sappho simply composed the whole thing as a dialogue between Alcaeus and herself.

83. The passage, without the name of its author, is quoted by Hephaestion (*Handbook of Meter* X. 4) as an example of a certain meter. Pausanias, however, in *Description of Greece* (IX. 29. 8), writes that Sappho was imitating the ancient Athenian hymn of Pamphos, in which Linus is called *Oetolinus*, or "Linus Dead."

The passage from Pausanias serves to demonstrate the way in which fragments come to be identified: "And Sappho of Lesbos, having learnt the name of 'Oetolinus' from the words of Pamphos, sang of Adonis and Oetolinus together."

On the basis of this remark it was possible to connect this fragment with Sappho, although there can be no certainty that Pausanias was referring specifically to the poem of this fragment.

89. In *Centuries of Proverbs* (I. 279), Diogenian quotes the lines as a proverb about someone who refuses the sweet things of life if having them requires that he take the painful ones too.

93. Maximus of Tyre, in *Dissertations* XVIII, quotes these lines as Sappho's to her daughter when the poetess was about to die.

98. Maximus, in *Dissertations* XVIII, 9d, quotes the lines to support his contention that as Prodicus, Gorgias, and Thrasymachus were rivals to Socrates, so were Gorgo and Andromache to Sappho. He says that the lines were addressed to one of them as a sarcasm.

101. Plutarch quotes this passage in his essay *On Restraining Anger* (VII) to fortify his argument, which reads: "A man who is silent over his wine is a burden to the company and a boor, whereas in anger there is nothing more dignified than tranquility . . ." (trans. J. M. Edmonds, *Lyra Graeca*, I, 277).

102. According to Maximus (*Dissertations* XVIII), Aphrodite addressed these words to Sappho.

111. This phrase probably derives from a cult song, or a song based on a cult song.

114. In *Dissertations* XVIII, Maximus says that in this fragment, and in fragment 129, Sappho is referring to Eros.

118. Certain liberties have been taken in the translation of this fragment. The text actually reads:

$$\beta\acute{\alpha}\rho\beta\iota\tau\text{os}.\ \ \beta\acute{\alpha}\rho\omega\mu\text{os}.\ \ \beta\acute{\alpha}\rho\mu\text{os}.$$

These three words refer to ancient stringed instruments deriving from oriental precursors. The *barbitos,* mentioned first, is usually translated "lyre," for all that is known about it is that it had a number of strings.

A literal translation into English forms would be meaningless to readers, who would be unable to associate any sound with the words. But changing the names of the instruments to those whose tonal qualities are familiar can create certain sense-associations for the modern reader.

GLOSSARY

Acheron. One of the rivers in the underworld which must be crossed by newly dead souls.

Adonis. A beautiful youth who was greatly loved by Aphrodite. In one story, when he was killed by a boar while hunting, Aphrodite made the red anemone spring from his blood. According to another story, Aphrodite gave him to Persephone to be brought up by her in the underworld. Persephone was reluctant to give him back, however, and it was arranged that he spend one-third of the year with her and two-thirds with Aphrodite.

Aelian (ca. A.D. 170–235). Roman author and teacher of rhetoric.

Alcaeus (born ca. 620 B.C.). Lyric poet of Lesbos, and a contemporary of Sappho.

Anactoria. A member of Sappho's circle.

Andromache. A princess of Thebe who became the wife of Hector in Troy.

Andromeda. A woman who may have held a position similar to that of Sappho in another such circle, and who was apparently Sappho's rival for the attentions of Atthis.

Aphrodite. The goddess of love and beauty. Sappho also refers to her as "Cypris" and "the Cyprian," after the island of Cyprus, onto which, according to one legend, she stepped after having risen out of the sea. (Most sources, however, hold the island to have been Cythera.) Aphrodite was the patron goddess of Sappho and her circle.

Apollo. The god of light, healing, music, poetry, archery, and prophecy.

Ares. The god of war.

Aristotle (384–322 B.C.). One of the greatest philosophers of antiquity, student of Plato, teacher of Alexander the Great, and author of a large body of writings covering most of the branches of philosophy, science, and rhetoric.

Athenaeus (A. D. 170–230). Greek scholar who was educated and lived in Alexandria. Athenaeus was the author of *Doctors at Dinner*, a 15-book compilation of classical references in the form of a dinner conversation between the most learned men of his day.

Atthis. A girl in Sappho's circle to whom a number of the poems are addressed. She was for some time very close to Sappho.

Calliope. The Muse of epic poetry.

Catullus (ca. 84–ca. 54 B.C.). Roman lyric and elegiac poet. Among his works are love poems written to the beautiful and notorious Clodia, in which he addresses her as "Lesbia" after Sappho. His poem 51 is an adaptation of Sappho's poem 8.

Cleis. The name of Sappho's mother and also of her daughter.

Crete. A large island in the Mediterranean Sea, south of the Cyclades.

Cypris. An epithet of Aphrodite (*q.v.*).

Cyprus. A large island in the Mediterranean Sea, south of Cilicia and west of Syria. (*See* Aphrodite.)

Cythera. An island southwest of the Peloponnesus, onto which Aphrodite is said to have stepped. Its inhabitants were noted for their worship of that goddess, and Sappho uses the epithet "Cytherea" in referring to her.

Demosthenes (384–322 B.C.). Famed Athenian orator.

Dika. The shortened form of the name Mnasidika (*q.v.*).

Diogenian. Greek grammarian of the middle 2nd century A.D.

Dionysius of Halicarnassus (30–8 B.C.). Rhetorician and historian at Rome; he wrote in Greek.

Doricha. The courtesan with whom Sappho's brother was said to have become involved, causing a scandal, when he was in Egypt. Herodotus tells the story in *Histories,* Bk. II, referring to her as Rhodopis, and Strabo, in his *Geography,* Bk. XVII, connects the two names.

Eos. The dawn goddess.

Eresus. A city of Lesbos, suggested as a possible birthplace of Sappho.

Eros. The god of love. According to one tradition he was among the oldest of the gods, and the comrade of Aphrodite; according to others, he was her son.

Gello. The Greek name for a child-stealing vampire or demoness, probably connected with the Semitic figure of Lilith and the Sumerian demon Gallu.

Gongyla. A member of Sappho's circle.

Gorgo. A member of Sappho's circle and possibly a rival of Sappho.

Graces. The three goddesses of grace and all that lends charm and beauty to life, called "Charites" by the Greeks.

Gyrinno. A member of Sappho's circle.

Hector. A prince of Troy, son of Priam and Hecuba, brother of Paris. Hector was the chief hero of Troy in the Trojan War, and was slain by Achilles. His marriage to Andromache is celebrated in poem 20.

Helen. Daughter of Zeus and Leda (or Nemesis, according to another tradition), said to be the most beautiful woman in the world. She was abducted from her husband Menelaus, in Sparta, by the Trojan prince Paris, thereby providing the ostensible cause of the Trojan War.

Hephaestion (fl. A.D. 150). An Alexandrian metrist, tutor of the Roman Emperor Verus, and author of a 48-book treatise entitled *Handbook of Meter.*

Hermes. The messenger of the gods and the guide of the dead to the underworld.

Hermogenes (born *ca.* A.D. 150). Greek rhetorician who wrote on the style and qualities of ancient authors.

Herodotus (484–ca. 428 B.C.). Greek historian whose writings are among the most important works of classical literature, containing information gleaned from his own travels and displaying a vast amount of geographical, historical, and literary knowledge.

Hesperus. The Evening Star.

Horace (65–8 B.C.). One of the most important poets of Augustan Rome. His *Odes* were greatly influenced by the Greek lyric poets, including Sappho, whose characteristic meter he used frequently.

Ida. A mountain in Asia Minor, near the city of Troy.

Ilus. The legendary founder of Troy, which was named for his father Tros and sometimes called after Ilus, as Ilium.

Irana. A member of Sappho's circle.

Leda. The wife of Tyndareus and mother of Castor and Pollux, Clytemnestra and Helen. She was approached by Zeus in the guise of a swan. There are differing versions of the story, attributing the four children to Tyndareus and Zeus in various combinations; and the egg (or two eggs), from which some of them are supposed to have sprung is considered in some versions to have been found and in others to have been laid.

Leto. The mother of Apollo and Artemis by Zeus.

Linus. A hero of ancient festivals held in Argos and Thebes. His death was connected with the annual decline of the crops in late summer and was mourned in chants sung by women and children.

Lydia. A district of Asia Minor, the seat of a wealthy and highly civilized people whose art and culture was influenced by, and in turn influenced, the Greeks.

Maximus of Tyre (ca. A.D. 125–185). Sophist and itinerant lecturer.

Medea. The daughter of Aeetes of Colchis. She loved and married Jason the Argonaut, and bore him two children, but was deceived by him. The story of her revenge is told by Euripides in his tragedy *Medea*.

Mnasidika. A member of Sappho's circle, sometimes called "Dika."

Muses. The nine deities of poetry, literature, dance, and music. They are the daughters of Zeus and Mnemosyne (Memory). Calliope is the Muse of epic poetry, Clio of history, Erato of lyric poetry, Euterpe of flutes, Melpomene of tragedy, Polymnia of mime, Terpsichore of dance, Thalia of comedy, and Urania of astronomy.

Mytilene (also Mitylene). The chief city of Lesbos, located on the eastern coast of the island, and one of the possible sites of Sappho's birth.

Nereids. The fifty (or one hundred) daughters of Nereus, an old sea god, and the sea nymph Doris. They lived with their father at the bottom of the sea.

Niobe. A woman whose twelve (or fourteen) children were killed by Apollo and Artemis because she boastfully compared herself to their mother Leto, who had only two children. She was traditionally depicted as a great stone figure eternally mourning her sons and daughters.

Paean. A name meaning "healer" applied to Apollo. The paean was originally a hymn sung to Apollo and derives its name from this epithet for him.

Palatine Anthology. A collection of Greek poetical epigrams compiled about A.D. 920.

Pamphos. A legendary poet of Attica, said to have preceded Homer.

Pandion. See note to poem 79.

Panormos. A place associated with the worship of Aphrodite.

The exact reference is in doubt, for there are several places that were so called: one in Sicily, one in Achaea, one on the east coast of Attica, one in Epirus, one on the north coast of Crete, and one in Ephesus.

Paphos. A city on the west coast of Cyprus, the site of a famous temple of Aphrodite.

Pausanias (fl. ca. A.D. 150). Greek geographer and traveler.

Peitho. The goddess of persuasion. The name is sometimes used to refer to another goddess, attendant on Aphrodite, and sometimes as an epithet for Aphrodite.

Persephone. The daughter of Zeus and Demeter. She was carried off to the underworld by Hades and spent part of the year there with him as his queen, and part of the year on the earth with her mother.

Pindar (518–438 B.C.). Lyric poet of Greece, known chiefly for his victory odes to athletes at the various games.

Placia. Seat of an ancient Pelasgian civilization, located near Mt. Olympus in northwest Asia Minor.

Plato (ca. 429–347 B.C.). Greek philosopher, student of Socrates, and teacher of Aristotle. He was the author of a large body of dialogues and some elegiac poetry.

Pleiades. Seven stars named for the daughters of Atlas who committed suicide and were turned to stars, according to one story, or were turned first to doves and then to stars, according to another. They are seen from the beginning of May until the beginning of November, and are associated with the fertilizing rains of spring, the seed time of autumn, and the autumn storms.

Plutarch (ca. A.D. 46–after 120). Academic philosopher and biographer, author of a large body of historiographical and critical literature.

Pollux (2nd century A.D.). Greek scholar and rhetorician.

Priam. The ruler of Troy during the Trojan War, and the father of many children, including Hector and Paris.

Sardis. The capital of Lydia (q.v.), and one of the most important ancient cities of Asia Minor.

Socrates (469–399 B.C.). Greek philosopher whose views on problems of ethics and knowledge were presented by his student Plato, in the latter's dialogues. No writings by Socrates himself are known to exist.

Solon (ca. 640–ca. 560 B.C.). Athenian legislator. He figured prominently in the rise of Athens to its position of importance among the Greek city-states. In addition to his fame as a lawgiver and military hero, he is highly regarded for his poetry.

Suidas. The name of a lexicon compiled about the end of the 10th century A.D.

Thebe. A city of Mysia in Asia Minor, and the birthplace of Andromache. It was sacked by Achilles and his men.

Timas. A member of Sappho's circle.

Tithonus. A son of Laomedon and brother of Priam. He was carried off by Eos on account of his beauty. She obtained for him the gift of immortality, but not eternal youth, and he became wrinkled and bent in his old age, and was finally transformed into a chirping cicada.

Zeus. The supreme Olympian god of the Greeks, the deity of thunder, lightning, law, royalty, travelers, and the household.

The Library of Liberal Arts